Additional Praise for *Synchronized Swimmers*

"The Painter's Garden" is the first piece in Tim Hawkins' latest book, and to me, that title is significant. When I imagine a painter's garden, I picture a place filled with beauty and memory, filled with the stuff of inspiration that leads to a greater and more nuanced view. The reader finds in *Synchronized Swimmers* a world that circles back upon itself, and though the paintings in that first work are "consumed by fire and forest," they still exist because we view them.

In this same way, memories that arise here continue to exist no matter how much time has passed. The memory of a father appears to be lost in the "frost-covered and locked" morgue entrance but is available in the "iridescent metal of starlings wheeling and calling in bright shafts of morning light." A sense of time seems freed from its moorings in these poems, and not only memories are free to move about, but other imaginings as well, all of these things accessible to us on the page, just as "all the dogs of his life will come running in from the countryside trailing their leashes, at long-last free to roam in feral, headlong packs."

—Jennifer Finstrom, poetry editor of *Eclectica Magazine* (2005–2018)

Hawkins, pen-to-paper, produces an intimate narrative that holds a mirror to the literal meaning of his words—precisely the mixture of Picasso and Gertrude Stein that he mentions in the flash fiction, "Things Have Dropped from Me." He is a poet and an artist, and his collection *Synchronized Swimmers* is deeply rooted and well crafted. The depth of his writing tangles me within the sturdy fabric of his style.

—Diana May-Waldman, award-winning journalist, author, activist, and poetry editor of *Blue Lake Review*

SYNCHRONIZED SWIMMERS

Poems and Stories by
TIM HAWKINS

Synchronized Swimmers
[Poems and Stories]
By Tim Hawkins

ISBN: 978-0-9980375-5-4

Publication date: October 2019

Published by KYSO Flash Press: www.kysoflash.com
Bellingham, Washington, USA. Printed in the USA.

Poems and stories in this collection are copyrighted by Tim Hawkins. All rights reserved. The majority of these works are reprinted from journals and magazines as listed under "Credits: First Publications" (see page 58).

This book was designed, edited, and produced by Clare MacQueen. The KYSO Flash logo is copyrighted © 2015 by Clare MacQueen and was designed in collaboration with James Fancher. All rights reserved.

Front and back covers designed by Clare MacQueen; background image is a cropped, tinted version of a black-and-white (B&W) photograph, *Hart Lake,* by Greg Shine (22 February 2017). Title-page image of Lake Louise is a B&W version of a color photograph by Jonathan Mueller (24 July 2011). For details, see photo credits on page 60. Both images are reproduced under Creative Commons license, Attribution 2.0 Generic (CC BY 2.0): https://creativecommons.org/licenses/by/2.0

Except for short quotations within critical articles or reviews, no portion of this book may be used, reproduced, or transmitted in any form or by any means, electronic or mechanical, including photocopying and recording, or by any information storage or retrieval system, without permission in writing from the Author.

Please send questions and comments to:

Author: tim.hawkins45@gmail.com

Publisher: KYSOWebmaster@gmail.com

Also by Tim Hawkins

Jeremiad Johnson
(In Case of Emergency Press, July 2019)

Wanderings at Deadline
(Aldrich Press, October 2012)

Dedication

To absent friends and those who left us too soon.

Above all, to Kathy, whose early departure leaves the largest void.

Kathleen Joy Hawkins Cole (1969–2016)

Table of Contents

11   The Painter's Garden
12   The Fibonacci Lawn
13   Southern Gothic
15   The Calm
17   Letter to a Distant Friend
19   Things Have Dropped From Me
21   Too Long in the Tropics
22   A Cold Autumn
23   This Animal
24   Oblivion
25   Overdue Rant
28   Still Life With Cocaine and Spiders
29   Taste
31   Vivid Dreams Again
32   An Offering
34   The Cold Space
35   Old School
36   The Dogs of His Life
37   The Premonition
40   Two Brothers
41   The Perfect Spiral
43   The Multitudes
44   Probity
45   Winter Thoughts
46   The Winter Sidewalks of Former Lovers
47   A Long Broken Passage
49   Pura Vida: An Alternative Travel Guide
52   Elegy Within Earshot of Howling
54   Synchronized Swimmers

57   About the Author
58   Credits: First Publications
60   Credits: Photographs
62   List of Poems and Stories in Alpha Order

Is it any wonder that strange personages occasionally visit these latitudes...? You might understand if a stranger looks away into the sun, before waving goodbye with arms that grow thinner each passing year.

[...]

The Painter's Garden

The garden of Doña Maria Flor del Campo verged on sumptuous wastefulness. Black squirrels fell from trees like the mangoes they consumed, sated on fermenting fruit in the hot morning sun. Fallen branches took root and grew in the fertile soil before becoming choked with lianas. The chortle of a stream marked a haphazard frontier with the looming rain forest, which Hector, the gardener, kept at bay with nothing more than machete and fire.

I sought her out on the advice of friends because of recurring nightmares and found the interior of her colonial house similarly overrun—by multitudes of canvases she had apparently labored over but was unable or unwilling to sell, piled at my feet like the dirty laundry of a lifetime of lovers.

It took several furtive inspections before I noticed incremental layers of dust, and I formed the impression that the piles comprised a chronological life's work. The entire retrospective might be catalogued by tipping the stacks like dominoes until the final canvas smacked linoleum, emitting an emphatic plume of dust.

"You must learn to practice forgiveness," she told me. The nightmares ceased and I returned several times for tea, though never quite suggested a journey through her life's work.

Afterward, Hector told me he had found her on a moonlit night, painting a large canvas in broad swatches of her own blood. I long for a photo of the garden and at least one of her paintings, but all was consumed by fire and forest.

The Fibonacci Lawn

Side by side the squares of grass grow smaller,

each revealing another hidden golden rectangle,

a homemade rendering of the Fibonacci sequence,
the length of some sides approaching the golden ratio,

as lap after lap he trudges behind the blasting
of the machine that vibrates in one hand
while the other cradles a jelly glass of bourbon.

Occasionally he sets the glass down on the square
to swat at a bee storm of the hand's own making
that only he can see and hear.
He imagines following the sequence
as far as the limits of his lawn will allow

the squaring of his spiraling thoughts,
and so, adjusts the blade to start again
with a larger square out where the sunflowers
have tumbled over the rundown cedar fence.
As the moon begins to rise, three children remain
watching in practiced silence from a window,
waiting for someone to notify them finally
that math class is dismissed.

Southern Gothic

Artifacts strewn and scattered among the ruins,
heaped alongside the teetering barn,
propped against fence posts with falling-down rails—
an iron rooster weather vane
divines the turmoil at our feet;
a rusted pump handle points the way
to a wood stove and spring house
set in dry creek beds run to mockery.

What are these things, the children ask?
And I hardly know how to answer,
for whatever I propose for this *mise-en-scène*
will never do it justice.

The one is for cooking biscuits, I say,
the other a cool place for black snakes
and spiders in the heat of day,
both anachronistic as the hand grinder,
the cotton gin, the Underwood typewriter,
the sweet smell of boxwoods and clover,
the loveliness of fresh mown hay...

But they've already lost interest
as other guests begin to arrive—
a rag man come to stitch a handmade doll;
a sharpener of knives all set to carve
a sheaf of silhouettes;
an unseen fox, perhaps, from up in the hills,
to scatter the plump due diligence of hens
while flightless turkeys roost on the splintered rails.

Luminous evening of honeysuckle and cornbread,
wisteria and magnolia blossom, please
bring forth the coolness of absolution, we pray.
For grasshoppers whir in barren fields
as hot and acrid as spit tobacco,
toads and all manner of creatures
are stymied and shrivel in the heat,
and dust rises for miles along the washboard road.

The Calm

We used to wonder at the old ones
and their refusal to pay us any mind;
at their reluctance to laugh at our escapades
and acknowledge our unique take on things.

Laughter for us was a spiraling out of control,
a momentous shift in the Earth's gravitational pull,
an invitation to a hair-raising frolic
in a lightning-stunned field.

While for them it was like a surprising concession
to put on a sweater, more of a slight change
in the weather than a storm.

And it wasn't just that way with laughter.
Everything for us was a spiraling out of control—
the first idea, the first desire, the first loss,
the first knowledge of the inevitable
sadness of things.

Now, I think I'm beginning to understand
why they walked so slowly from the mailbox
with letters and cards and the sun in their arms,
why they seemed to be searching
for someone lost
deep inside the mirror,
and why they enjoyed the soft clatter
of washing dishes together, talking
in the glow of the setting sun.

I am unable to forget
how they disappeared quietly,
one-by-one,
though their occasional words
inhabit the wisteria, the porch swing
and the railing.

Sometimes, on Sunday evenings,
I drive for miles through the twilight,
searching for their faces
and listening for their words
and soft laughter
on the front porches
of every small town.

Letter to a Distant Friend

A sack of coffee freshly roasted,
socked away among a couple of loaves,
and on the stove a pan
ready for steaming milk;

not much else,
a bit of cheese, some drops of oil.

But to have this, the potential
for another few contented hours,
I'm beginning to understand
why you kept your things so closely guarded,

and why you lingered so
in the delight of preparation;

how folding socks was no chore
and tea could be made
only with your full attention;

how much you expressed
in the deliberate pauses we took for granted
as an excuse to smoke.

"I want to write…because I love making things,"
you admitted once, pausing to light another one
as we awaited the craft of your storytelling.

Forgive me for bumming smokes
and for asking:

Where is it?
What have you made?

At your leisure, when you are ready,
make me a poem of peach pie
or Hong Kong girls walking arm-in-arm
on a warm harbor night.

And after some reflection I will fix coffee,
taking in the full measure
with all deliberate haste.

Things Have Dropped From Me

—for Marianne Edwards

And, like Virginia Woolf, I too have outlived certain desires...and I too have lost friends. One gorgeous, halcyon friendship in particular with a young woman whose face elicits a flood of rain-filled streets I was not then afraid to cross. I have that face not only emblazoned in memory, but also inscribed into a dozen sketch pads, for she often sat for me on a stool near the window where the raging moonlight flooded my studio apartment. One night, in particular, she read aloud from *The Waves* as I sketched.

We were both alone and new to the city. We lived across the hall and slipped passages of mad scribbling under one another's doors at daylight, flushed and feverish from a night's work. She was a real poet, and I was just beginning to feel I had earned the right to call myself a painter. This friend was one of the few I trusted to cast a critical eye at my work. How I painted to please that eye! And wrote atrocious poems for that sleep-filled eye, and met its gaze peering over a coffee cup at me, and later looked and looked for it in a crowd at some of my early shows, and later in the posh and trendy galleries. But I lost that friend because she made a simple gesture I could not return.

Several years after we both moved out of the city, she dedicated her first book of poetry to me. Instead of sending an instant thank you or making a long-distance call, I began to believe I had to make a grand gesture in return; a gesture not just of thanks, but something that would make me worthy of her gesture. Why? Because I was a struggling painter and a young wife and had received no accolades, only the kind reassurance of her clear eye and unvarnished opinions. So, I put off responding until I had made my own success. In the interim I invented all kinds of scenarios—we were Picasso and Gertrude Stein in a famous feud;

we were bound to run into one another one day; I was going to dedicate my first show to her. But we weren't really feuding and I didn't have my first show for another ten years; my modest success came rather late. I never spoke to her again.

Her gorgeous life gradually loosened and dropped silently from mine. When I heard that she had died, the grief was only incrementally more than I'd felt each time I thought of her in the last 35 years. To give this tragedy some meaning, I now tell myself there are some friends, people whom one wants to preserve in memory as one remembers them, changeless, smiling, young and fearless. These are friends one wishes to never grow old, so one kills them young and they die full of glory. This is what I wish to believe so that my behavior has some semblance of reason—as if reason ever justified killing the thing you love.

Editor's Note: "Things have dropped from me. I have outlived certain desires; I have lost friends, some by death…others through sheer inability to cross the street" is spoken by the character Bernard in *The Waves* (Hogarth Press, United Kingdom, 1931; page 132) by British novelist, essayist, and critic Virginia Woolf (1882–1941).

Too Long in the Tropics

Hammocks and beer and lassitude can only get you so far.
One longs to feel a distinction between mind and body,
between body and air, to know a separation,
that here stands an individual
human, birch, maple or otherwise:
limbs trembling in the autumn dusk;
corn stalks, cattails and fallow fields,
brown underbrush, frost and crows in the half-light;
pine cones, thistles and burning stars,
breath visible, the memory of breath visible,
anticipation and exhalation,
sweaters and sweaters coming off;
off seasons—a lonely baseball diamond,
a swirling wind kicking up scraps in the dugout,
harsh landscapes and the anticipation of change;
growth rings, subsiding and decline,
a definite sense of departure, people and seasons
not just fading from sight;
rubbing one's hands together,
and this time not in anticipation, but for survival;
hard water, chapped skin, chapped lips,
and not from kissing, but from neglect.

Oh, but have I mentioned how clear
and how cold it can be under the stars?
And the snowfall among the pines?

A Cold Autumn

The last time we spoke was deep in the cold autumn of 1973, in front of a shuttered store on Front Street. I found him brushing crumbs from the lapel of his corduroy jacket with one hand and brandishing a crust of bread in the other. Tall and thin, with curly dark hair and horn-rimmed glasses, he appeared intense and scholarly from across the road. Nose-to-nose, however, I could see desperation in his eyes and spittle at the corner of his mouth. He tried to hold onto a coherent thought while asking me for money. I, his only son, turned him down and walked away.

When he was found near the railroad crossing east of town, I was the one they called. The side entrance to the morgue was frost-covered and locked, but I remember turning to face the iridescent metal of starlings wheeling and calling in bright shafts of morning light.

This Animal

When I realize Mike won't be getting back up, I turn toward a casino doorway of angry, frightened faces, searching for recognition as a fellow human being, as a baseball fan, as a betting man. Finally I'll settle for recognition as a drunken brute, but even this seems to be asking too much. Nobody says anything. This animal turns on its tentative, uncertain feet and staggers away, shape-shifting and looking for places to hide. This animal scurries along with tail tucked firmly between its legs, skittish and growling, shying away from human contact like a coyote with a gnawed-off leg.

Oblivion

To the muskrat and deer
I am stone in the sun-dappled riffle;
only the heron, always one river bend ahead,
still recognizes me as human.

Overdue Rant

My landlady has the gift of second sight and likes to talk politics.
She tells me that Reagan saved Central America
from communism, then she raves about the dead Vietnamese
while extolling Somoza's reforms. She cooks herself
six meals a day and offers me moldy grapes.
When her pots and pans have gathered flies for six days
she curses the sick maid and reminds me to wash my plate.
Jesus made her invisible on a bus ride through El Salvador
where she had gone to tidy her late brother's affairs.
He died of a broken appendix;
hoarding toilet paper did him no good.
I have rationed my rice, and when I'm hungry it is gone.
She keeps fish heads in the refrigerator for the cat.
My eggs smell like fish heads, my cheese smells like fish heads,
my rice smells like fish heads and is gone.
She has invited me to a gathering of sober Americans abroad
on my day off.

She was a starving actress in the Sixties,
and is now a painter of some reputation.
She holds her new grandson close to her breast
while his father raises his voice.
She was beautiful then, and I believe her.
Now she holds her grandson close to her breast like a ham.
She had a Hollywood contract and filmed half a picture.
She was raven-haired and played the part of Rebecca.
The Actor's Studio was so taken with her "suicide"
she was auctioned off like a side of beef.
In a fit of pride she returned to Costa Rica
and became a landlady.

She is a good landlady, although she sometimes forgets
to properly store her perishables.
She has only burned the house down once.

Some producer was coming down to fetch her on his yacht.
He was taken with her innocence, but liked to call her "grandma,"
since she was all of twenty-two.
He set sail from Miami with a crew of six,
ranging in age from thirteen to fourteen,
and inevitably died of a heart attack.
The panic-stricken girls left his body to rot on deck,
afraid they'd be accused of murder
if they nudged his stiff corpse over the side
with their still-growing feet.
For days they subsisted on brandy and cigars,
drifting in an aimless frenzy along the Gulf Stream,
a feast of gulls pounding the cabin door…

You never told me how it ended, though
it is safe to assume they were rescued, I suppose.
Forgive me now for this intrusion.
I have just now come upon this after all these years;
I believe I wrote it the first time my rent was late
when I hardly knew you at all,
before I learned Spanish on the tape recorder and
your voice had become to me
the breathless epiphanies of Lorca and Neruda.
I finish it now ten years down the line,
many years since I have lost the tapes
and a long time since I was your friend.

Synchronized Swimmers | 27

Blur

Still Life With Cocaine and Spiders

The spiders woven in crepuscular shadows,
aloof in their invited webs,
coked to the gills in amber
on insect adrenaline
drained from a thousand holes.

The weightless husks of the discarded
like my apologies dropped to the floor,
stepped on and grinning
in their fossil reincarnations.

This is our home: interior design
courtesy of Munch,
silent narrator of
the end of the weekend,
stairways cloaked in gray morning light
and insects cringing from the door.

Doubled over like unmade beds,
each new week unmade with shaking hands,
like those high-climbing insects
we are on the relentless cusp
of something like fame or death,

while spiders dream
in gossamer webs
in the bloodstained windows of dawn.

Taste

Her first gift to me was the gilt-framed landscape photograph that reminds me of one of my grandmother's jigsaw puzzles she kept stashed in her closet to ward off a rainy day. Residing in three hinged sections—an anonymous mountain, picturesque yet mundane in its grandeur, vaulting into an impossibly blue airbrushed sky, and a symmetrical stand of pines in the foreground as lifelike as train-set accessories. There might even be an eagle or two flying around. The thought that passes through my mind is, "at least it matches the couch."

As art, I wouldn't quite know how to categorize it, and I suppose neither would she. She's never heard of Romanticism, the Pre-Raphaelites, or Abstract Expressionism, and yet tonight as we walk home from the movie she speaks of the night breeze lifting her soul up to the sky.

Next came the ceramic figures; first singly, then, as if to the ark, in pairs. The first was an enormous black bull, his comic member nearly dragging the ground. What to do with such a thing? She suggested the coffee table, but I tactfully mentioned my concern about friends and their large drunken feet. The dusty shelves of the spare bedroom, I felt, might provide a more discreet curio cabinet. We compromised on the living room shelves, and *Being and Nothingness, Critique of Pure Reason,* and *An Essay Concerning Human Understanding* now live out their natural, unread lives in the spare bedroom.

Later came the swans, each wearing the kind of corsage that you might have expected your great-aunt Edna to have lost in the back seat of a 1947 Packard; each with the painted eyes of a carnival barker suggesting with a wink, "I know this is rigged, but you bought the ticket." Come to think of it, they look like the kind of prize you might expect to win for knocking over a milk bottle or popping three balloons. Those same eyes seem to be laughing at me, implying, "You won me. Now what the hell are you going to do with me?"

Judging from her mother's living room, which includes a transparent nude wrapped around an ashtray and a velvet *Madonna and Child*, I'm sure there are other such gifts to come. But I don't mind. Tonight, she dances merengue and salsa around the apartment, oblivious to my so-called trappings of good taste: the Vermeer print, the Tang Dynasty watercolor, the beer-can ashtrays littering the coffee table.

Tonight, with her soul in the sky, she dances only for me, somewhere between the bull, the swans, and the mountain.

Vivid Dreams Again

Sleep is the cat above the bed
peering down through the broken ceiling tile.

(the floor swirls with carp. . . and she pounces)

Sleep is the abandoned house
where we danced in one dry corner
for a solid year.

Sleep is the raincoat
of kisses we wore,
sleek and wet
in that house of monsoons.

Sleep is the hard welcome rain
that comes at daylight.

Hack the vines from the walls.
Uncoil the snakes from the kettle.
Peel the snails from your eyes.
Wake to the white-hot afternoon.

An Offering

Do you remember the hour
you tumbled naked, headlong
out of sleep and the burning sky?

You found yourself, frail and stumbling
in a landscape of bone and tumbling waters,
picking berries alone,

wandering from thicket to thicket
as the juice ran in crimson tears
from the corners of your smile.

This is all I need of you:
an offering of words, like berries
collected in the loneliest hour of that day.

Whisper some small true words
not spit from the mouths
of friends,
not coughed out gasping
from another life.

Whisper some small true words
bearing the scars of your teeth and
we shall savor the harvest with our tongues.

Offer your gathering of summer storms,
or the branches trembling in your winter sky.
Offer the night moving in you.

Make an offering
of the silences roaring within
and we shall have no more need of words.

We will share
armloads or mouthfuls
of any berry you like,

first gathered in days of rage,
ripened and burning like skin,
then cooled in night-blooming silence.

The Cold Space

Leaving
her warmth, the dark
morning chill on his skin,
the cold space he has created
remains.

Old School

Nobody in our Midwestern town would have admitted to seeing a psychiatrist. "Psycho, nut job, loon" were terms thrown freely about, only a few years removed from Eagleton's ambitions derailed by electroshock and Muskie's presidential bid coming unglued by his tears. Those were the days when Nixon slept in a suit and tie, though he made the concession to Pat of untying his shoelaces before crawling into bed. Many of us still grieve for those old-school dads who quietly and discreetly gave themselves coronaries, drank themselves to death, or blew their brains out rather than simply admit to human frailty and need.

The Dogs of His Life

Amid all the sighing, the tears and the waiting,
the unreal balance of boredom and dread
in the restless pacing of his next of kin,

a melee ensues from under the covers—

a dispossessed hamlet of sunken peripheries
and imploding contours, where the windswept rattle
and rust of decay are the only signs of industry.

Soon, all the dogs of his life will come running in
from the countryside trailing their leashes, at long-last
free to roam in feral, headlong packs; while long-lost loves

sit gently at the bedside, stroking the velvet muzzles
and ears of chestnut horses, a family of distant travelers
wandering in from a forgotten summer's day.

The Premonition

—for Sam

It's raining tonight, on Halloween,

and three little neighborhood boys
(Spiderman, a wizard, a clown)
and their mothers have stopped by
to trick or treat and to ask:
"How do you say that in Spanish?"

"*Dulces o travesuras*," pipes up my three-year-old daughter,
playing to the crowd with just some of the many gifts
    at her disposal—
the unusual admixture of several native tongues,
two sparkling black eyes,
and those bountiful curls that are graced by a crown,
for tonight she is dressed, appropriately enough,
as the princess of all mermaids.

Like all fathers of great beauties
I have my biases and blind spots
and my vague hopes and fears,
but tonight I see clearly the great joy
and pain that this beauty will bring.

It's raining tonight, on Halloween.

Someday soon, after the masks have been put away
and children have grown tired and restless
or sick on their sweets,
this night will recede into little more
than a photograph or an anecdote,

and a vague and stormy memory
of the time her father foretold the future.

Synchronized Swimmers | 39

Wade

Two Brothers

—for Chey

The west wind blows his rail-thin silhouette
slouching back to town as Halloween
fades, scattering my middle-class pieties
like discarded wrappers at the children's feet.

He gnaws on domesticity like a bone,
leaving gristle on my lumpy sofa bed,
humoring my good intentions like a faithful dog
who would eat his way through you for his freedom.

At some point, as frost gathers on the horizon,
I begin to mutter about values and hard choices,
though, occasionally, I too, long to sleep in contentment
beneath the piano, or to wake with leaves in my hair.

Then, just like that, without a word he sets off again, the children
with fewer tears and questions as they grow accustomed,
and I, with no reliable information
about where he sleeps tonight.

Many possibilities—alleys and boxcars
or wrapped in plastic out beneath the pines—
though I try hard not to imagine.

Instead, I settle for tossing and turning,
playing the piano, and contemplating
sleeping in late from time to time.

The Perfect Spiral

—for Gibby

Throwing a football with my son
who's just getting old enough to catch and throw
a tight spiral, in the gathering dusk,
under a street lamp, hazy
with the smoke of burning leaves,
as the bone-chilling cold of late November
collides with the pleasure of these things,

I'm reminded of those same November evenings
of my youth, when we played in such a fever
that we could somehow see the ball
long after dark, without feeling the cold,
without hearing the voices
that called us home to that other
brightly-lit world of expectation.

Tonight, a family of evangelical missionaries—
a father and mother, with two shivering
ill-suited boys in tow—
puts a temporary halt to our game,
the father preaching gloomy, eternal life
with an exhortation, a warning of sorts
that I must be born again.

For the sake of the boys, or perhaps
because I already feel November-born again,
I refrain from the easy sarcasm that
has become my stock, first-down play.

I long to show them, instead, the sacred gift
of night vision, and the flashes of eternity
that inhere like slow motion
in a moment of artful concentration.

I offer him my own invitation, of sorts,
by tossing him the ball without a word.
We could achieve miracles here in the dark,
leading one another just enough
out past the clothesline, making leaping grabs
by feel, each a hero to our boys
amid cheers and shouts echoing through the night,
with no talk of damnation
or angelic hosts on high.

But he has become a man and
has put away childish things, so he
flips me the ball with a shake of the head,
then leads the family away on their
eternal rounds through the gloom,
shivering and groping blindly toward the light.

We, the damned, have slipped through their grasp
and return easily to our perfect spirals
and death-defying grabs,
while ignoring the cold,
and the dark, faceless silhouette
that has magically appeared
in a burst of light at the window
to beckon us home for the night.

The Multitudes

A frenzy of starlings sweeps through the plaza—
they soar past the bridge and redouble their flight,
a dervish that whirls past the invisible homeless,
then finally settles in to roost for the night—
while peregrine falcons watch from two steeples,
a Catholic and Lutheran ecumenical feast.
These multitudes flourish and never diminish,
a marvel akin to the loaves and the fishes,
as miraculous to some as the wine and the Host.
But the churches have shut their doors to the plight
of the homeless who sleep beneath the two bridges,
and the colony alights with a sound much like laughter
in the throat of the night where they take up their post.

Probity

The black
robes of justice
hang on the chamber door,
dripping with honor, probity,
and rain.

Rogue River

Winter Thoughts

> If anyone on the verge of action should judge himself according to the outcome, he would never begin.
>
> —Søren Kierkegaard, *Fear and Trembling*

Others no longer present have traced fitting inscriptions into the steam of the window and the dust of the bureau: *Flat Affect; Bent, Not Broken; White Knuckling It; The Starving Time; A God-Awful Thing to Behold.* They could attest to a flash-frozen landscape out there—all cold casks of herring in an ice-covered brine. Beyond the window I hear and envision the clop-clop of ragged ponies leading ethereal funeral processions down stark and abandoned boulevards lined with gray and leafless trees.

Off in the distance, forever out of reach, Kierkegaard, or someone like him, makes his way through the drifts, dragging his club foot, crablike, on spindly legs, hunched over in thought and holding fast to his quicksilver notions, as eternal in the gray northern twilight as they are nearly invisible. Barely keeping his feet, he seems from this vantage the fleeting, black shadow of a crow.

Perhaps, when all is written, no stoic horses will have wintered, trembling, in these fields. And perhaps, after all, it was *not* Kierkegaard who wrote of winter that it is: "The untimely intrusion of grand, bleak, monolithic eternity on the ephemeral consciousness, like an animal that finds its gaze in the black current of a slow-moving river, and holds steadfastly to it, never looking away, until it freezes over and becomes opaque, then clouds over with snow." But friend, there are so many things I could tell you, so many tasks I would undertake, once winter is truly over.

Editor's Note: Epigraph as translated by Alastair Hannay (Penguin Books, 1985)

The Winter Sidewalks of Former Lovers

Like winter itself,
slick and sudden as an ice patch,
barren as a field of broken stalks,

a moment arrives,
as familiar and forgotten
as the solstice,
bearing with it
the wind-chill factor
on the year's coldest day.

In the face of this front,
occasioned by flurries
and frostbit shrugs,

hands clench eloquently in pockets
and words break like icicles.

We hold our ground
as if working to steady
two diverging floes of ice,

trying one boot for balance
and then the other,
until finally, in the thaw of silence
we see our own breath
and realize we are dancing alone.

A Long Broken Passage

On horseback, at night, winding slowly skyward
through dry-season wash, amid outcropping boulders,
past sluggish, latent rattlesnake, hibernacula of lizard,
stars so near at hand, so crystalline,
so close to the mountain I can reach up
and cut my wrists on their jagged contours.

I feel the warmth of the horse pass through me;
our steady exhalations rise as one.

Not far off a wildcat screams,
flushing a covey of night-roosting doves.
A whirlwind, the clatter of hooves on stone,
and yet my horse remains composed.
Steadfast, she gathers herself beneath me.

Sitting alone, above it all, rocking toward the heavens,
my cold, shaking hand strokes the side of her neck
as if reaching into a rushing current.
I imagine that over the next dark ridge
we will come to a sudden halt,
face-to-face with a bold white horse
in the sagebrush-scented moonlight.

It is a long broken passage back down
to the land of all things familiar, back down
to the smell of oats and dust and manure.

The game birds, the reptiles, the horse and I,
the stars—we all must die. We know this.
But since I know so little of wildcats
or white horses for that matter,
and dust does not rely on timely arrivals,
we may tarry for just a while longer
among the sagebrush and boulders.

Pura Vida: An Alternative Travel Guide

Part of a dense and varied isthmus, riotous, overgrown with lianas, epiphytes, and creeping vines; verdant, lush, and fragrant in absurd amounts, seemingly as tall as wide, Costa Rica's mountains push a fertile volcanic soil toward the sky. Each voracious caress by sun and rain brings forth a teeming splendor from the earth, where heaving native rock is overthrown by bounding thickets of rebirth and decay.

The children of other continents, who attempted to settle the land, trekked upward into dark cloud forest, cutting, cleaving, and hacking as they went, through rot and fungus, amid strange screaming sounds, laden like oxen with brutally heavy loads, wary of stinging insects, venomous snakes, and marauding jungle cats; dripping with humid perspiration, dying in childbirth, dying of infected wounds, dying of malaria and other tropical fevers, dying of loneliness and fear.

You can meet the descendants of these rugged settlers in every town. Santa Maria de Dota lies in a high valley of the *Cordillera de Talamanca*. Renowned for its coffee, breathtaking vistas, and abundance of fauna, the village's iconic church is found near the cemetery where ten-year-old Asunción Castro has thrown himself sobbing onto his mother's grave and fallen into a deep and haunted sleep. Nobody dares move him for days, through wind and sun and rain. In these latitudes, Asunción survives the exposure, but staggers home to his sisters a vastly different boy.

You may have heard the story of Chito the Crocodile Man, a fisherman from Siquirres, who kisses, embraces, swims, and sleeps with a crocodile he nursed back to health. Do not, under any circumstance, be tempted to try this.

But do make sure to visit San Antonio de Escazú, where the *vaquero* Don Miguel wears his señora's clothing to the *fiesta de boyero*. Five long years have passed since Doña Carmen paused to catch her breath in the doorway, collapsing there amid a clattering armload of sticks, and today he wears her white cotton dress with blue trim to the running of the bulls. He won't ever stop wearing her garments, he says, until his dust is mingled with hers.

Is it any wonder that strange personages occasionally visit these latitudes, leaving only unrecorded observations and perfectly round pre-Colombian spheres? You might understand if a stranger looks away into the sun, before waving goodbye with arms that grow thinner each passing year.

Forgive me if you already know this, but the golden toad once inhabited the elfin cloud forest of Monteverde, especially along a cold wet ridge called Brillante. They laid their eggs in rainwater pools among tree roots and bromeliads. The last documented sighting occurred in 1989.

Anyway, don't forget to visit the central plaza of Guapiles, where Mariela de los Angeles accompanies her favorite uncle who likes to buy her dresses and *confites*. On a hot afternoon, she waits with pleasant anticipation as he buys them a cold drink of *pipa* served with straws in a plastic bag. Popular, confident, and smiling, he greets those he knows by name, pausing to chat before disappearing from sight, cut down by the machete of a drunken friend.

Mariela steals away in silence before the gathering crowd can confirm what she already knows. On the way to her village, fish from the cold mountain stream clean the *granos* from Mariela's feet, as her tears dry in the dust of her cheeks. Two of her younger brothers patiently wait, kicking a makeshift ball while she tries to call a *yigüirro* down from the mango tree where it looks to flush a singular worm from the globes of dense orange fruit.

Unsuccessful, though laden with mangoes, the three hike back to the mountain, leaving behind the distant memory of gathering crowds. At the last turnoff, before gravel gives way to mud, then narrows into well-worn jungle path, they are joined by three writhing snakes and a dead horse burning on the side of the road.

When they arrive at the gossip of the cooking fires, a cousin in the next village is said to have been devoured by a feral sow, and the baby, Juan Carlos, has died of worms. They say nothing with respect to their uncle. What, after all, is there to say?

Consumed by the humid fullness of the rain forest and the tropical night, is it any wonder that spirits of jaguars and departed souls are regularly encountered? Is it any wonder that strange personages occasionally visit these latitudes, leaving only unrecorded observations and perfectly round pre-Colombian spheres?

Forgive me if you already know this: The forest floor is composed of distinct levels of decomposition merging into one indistinguishable mass—immutable terror, the acid adrenaline of shock, unearthed regret, and final insect entitlement, stripped of embellishment, stripped to the bone.

Next time I will tell you more about the few remaining original inhabitants. But for now, tales of the settlers whose blood mingled with theirs will have to suffice. You told me you sought an authentic Central American vacation experience. Forgive me for pointing this out with arms that grow thinner each passing year, but the golden toad is gone, while the dead horse burns along the roadside as the worm turns just out of reach of the national bird in the mango's sweet orange flesh.

Elegy Within Earshot of Howling

—for Todd Tubergen

Returning from a family birding trip to Manistee,
I finally found your grave after all these years.

About to give up in my third pass through the small country cemetery,
I caught my breath as I literally stumbled upon your name.

Like you, the marker was slightly off kilter,
and, as if in deference to the memory of your style,
it wore the five o'clock shadow of a decade of wind and rain.

My four-year-old ran laughing around your stone
while his older brother doled out harsh glares and whispers
of reprimand, until I patted him on the shoulder to say it was all right.

As we stood there in the midst of that sweet laughter
and the beginnings of a soft spring rain,
I remembered the last time we spoke on the phone,
very near the end, when you invoked Rilke:

> "Take the emptiness you hold in your arms
> and scatter it into the open spaces we breathe:
> maybe the birds will feel how the air is thinner
> and fly with more affection…"

and announced your love for all
the youthful, scattered days of our friendship
when we ran from place to place, from one illicit dawn to the next,
down to the continent's edge
to shout wild oaths and promises.

Your voice was so thin and rasping,
it foretold, without proclaiming, the inevitable,
so different than what we had promised and imagined.
"Beauty is nothing but the beginning of terror, which we are still
 just able to endure,"
I somehow managed to respond.

When we hung up that last time, my wife held me down
as I howled and raged on my hands and knees
all across the cold, hard tiles of that floor on another continent,
as worms crawled beneath the foundation of our house
and stars blazed outside in the night sky.

For a while I tried to follow your advice,
and even pledged to serenade
each of the mornings after you died
with some form or another
of my ragged and lusty song.

But my voice has grown hoarse, and I am forgetful—
still I'm aware of some of what remains,
aware now that I've set up camp, without even knowing it,
in the proximity of birds, and within earshot of that howling,
with ready and certain access to the reverberations of its call.

Editor's Note: Quotations are from Rainer Maria Rilke's "First Elegy": (1) "Take the emptiness you hold..." is from *The Duino Elegies*, translated from the German by Gary Miranda (Tavern Books, 2013); and (2) "[For] beauty is nothing..." is from *The Duino Elegies and the Sonnets to Orpheus*, translated by Stephen Mitchell (Vintage, 2009).

Synchronized Swimmers

—for Ilsy

On a night such as this,
with the windows open wide,
in a stream of moonlight
and the air warm as blood,
we find ourselves crawling toward something,
tossing and turning, hip and flank churning;
if we stop moving we will drown, it seems,
yet the moon draws no closer.

We come together briefly
as if meeting out in the deep,
kicking gently, careful not to drag
one another down.

Toward morning there may come
troubling dreams
as all around us countless feed.
But until then, floating on our backs
near the calm, warm surface of this marriage
of water and air,
there is the night-blooming
fragrance of honeysuckle
and we are buoyant and enveloped,
uncertain where one ends and the other begins.

Llandanwg Beach

Whisper some small true words...

About the Author

Tim Hawkins lives with his wife and three children in his hometown of Grand Rapids, Michigan, where he works in communications in the health care and biomedical research industry. In his younger days, he worked his way through high school, college, and afterward at a host of jobs including dishwasher, busboy, fry cook, waiter, bartender, landscaper, house painter, door-to-door canvasser, telemarketer, taxi driver, soap factory line worker, Alaskan fish cannery slime-table worker, stevedore, nose-hair clipper model, and Taiwan cram-school teacher. After graduating from University of Michigan, he worked his way around the world for the better part of two decades, studying the Spanish and Chinese languages and working as a journalist, technical writer, grant writer, adjunct professor, and teacher in international schools.

To date, more than 200 of his works of short fiction, nonfiction, and poetry have been published in 40+ print and online magazines and anthologies, including *Blueline, Eclectica, Iron Horse Literary Review, KYSO Flash, The Midwest Quarterly, The Pedestal Magazine, The Shit Creek Review, Tipton Poetry Journal,* and *Valparaiso Poetry Review.* His work has been nominated for the Pushcart Prize, *Best of the Net* (Sundress Publications), and *Best Microfiction,* and he served as preliminary judge for the 47th Annual Dyer-Ives Poetry Competition (2015) judged by Mark Doty. Tim's debut poetry collection, *Wanderings at Deadline,* was published in 2012 by Aldrich Press. In July 2019, In Case of Emergency Press published his chapbook *Jeremiad Johnson.*

Find out more at his website: www.timhawkinspoetry.com

Credits: First Publications

- A Cold Autumn [a slightly different version] / *Ad Hoc Fiction* (28 February 2018)
- A Long Broken Passage / *KYSO Flash* (Issue 11, Spring 2019)
- An Offering / *Blue Lake Review* (April 2019)
- Elegy Within Earshot of Howling / *Eclectica* (Vol. 16, No. 2, April/May 2012); nominated by *KYSO Flash* for the Pushcart Prize
- Letter to a Distant Friend / *Sixfold* (Summer 2013)
- Oblivion / *Shot Glass Journal* (Issue 7, May 2012)
- Old School / *KYSO Flash* (Issue 12, September 2019)
- Overdue Rant / *The Literary Bohemian* (Issue 2, December 2008)
- Probity / *Shot Glass Journal* (Issue 7, May 2012)
- Pura Vida: An Alternative Travel Guide / *KYSO Flash* (Issue 8, August 2017)
- Southern Gothic / *Valparaiso Poetry Review* (Vol. XIX, No. 2, Spring/Summer 2018)
- Synchronized Swimmers / *KYSO Flash* (Issue 11, Spring 2019)
- Taste / *KYSO Flash* (Issue 12, September 2019)
- The Calm [a slightly different version] / *Eclectica* (Vol. 23, No. 1, January/February 2019)
- The Cold Space / *Sketchbook: A Journal for Eastern and Western Short Forms* (Vol. 6, No. 3, 27 July 2011)
- The Dogs of His Life / *KYSO Flash* (Issue 12, September 2019)
- The Fibonacci Lawn [a slightly different version] / *The Fib Review* (Issue 7, August 2010)
- The Multitudes / *KYSO Flash* (Issue 12, September 2019)
- The Painter's Garden / *Flash Frontier* (June 2017: Journeys)
- The Perfect Spiral / *Umbrella: A Journal of Poetry and Kindred Prose* (Issue 6, Spring 2008)
- The Premonition / *Underground Voices Magazine* (February 2012)

- The Winter Sidewalks of Former Lovers [an early version: four-line micro-poem] / *Eunoia Review* (20 November 2011)
- Things Have Dropped From Me / *KYSO Flash* (Issue 9, Spring 2018)
- This Animal / *Dogzplot* (December 2014)
- Too Long in the Tropics / *Visitant* (29 May 2019)
- Two Brothers / *KYSO Flash* (Issue 11, Spring 2019), which nominated the poem for Sundress Publications' *Best of the Net Anthology*
- Winter Thoughts [a slightly different version] / *Unbroken Journal* (Issue 20, January 2019)

- *Ad Hoc Fiction*: A Cold Autumn
- *Blue Lake Review*: An Offering
- *Dogzplot*: This Animal
- *Eclectica*: Elegy Within Earshot of Howling; The Calm
- *Eunoia Review*: The Winter Sidewalks of Former Lovers [an early version: four-line micro-poem]
- *Flash Frontier*: The Painter's Garden
- *KYSO Flash*: A Long Broken Passage; Old School; Pura Vida: An Alternative Travel Guide; Synchronized Swimmers; Taste; The Dogs of His Life; The Multitudes; Things Have Dropped From Me; Two Brothers
- *Shot Glass Journal*: Oblivion; Probity
- *Sixfold*: Letter to a Distant Friend
- *Sketchbook (A Journal for Eastern and Western Short Forms)*: The Cold Space
- *The Fib Review*: The Fibonacci Lawn
- *The Literary Bohemian*: Overdue Rant
- *Umbrella (A Journal of Poetry and Kindred Prose)*: The Perfect Spiral
- *Unbroken Journal*: Winter Thoughts
- *Underground Voices Magazine*: The Premonition
- *Valparaiso Poetry Review*: Southern Gothic
- *Visitant*: Too Long in the Tropics

Credits: Photographs

- Cover (designed by Clare MacQueen): *Hart Lake* (near Warner Wetlands ACEC), a cropped and tinted version of a black-and-white (B&W) photograph of a Canada goose on the wing near a bevy of swans, by Greg Shine, Bureau of Land Management (22 February 2017); reproduced under Creative Commons license, Attribution 2.0 Generic (CC BY 2.0):

  https://creativecommons.org/licenses/by/2.0

- Title Page: *Lake Louise* (Banff National Park, Alberta, Canada), B&W version of a color photograph by Jonathan Mueller (24 July 2011); reproduced under Creative Commons license, Attribution 2.0 Generic (CC BY 2.0):

  https://creativecommons.org/licenses/by/2.0

- Page 27: *Blur*, B&W photograph by GW, of thatch palm during windstorm in the Florida Keys (3 January 2018); reproduced under Creative Commons license, Public Domain Mark 1.0:

  https://creativecommons.org/publicdomain/mark/1.0/

- Page 39: *Wade*, sepia photograph by Ben Seidelman (24 May 2016); reproduced under Creative Commons license, Attribution 2.0 Generic (CC BY 2.0):

  https://creativecommons.org/licenses/by/2.0/legalcode

- Page 44: *Rogue River* (winter in Rockford, Michigan), cropped version of photograph by Ilsy Murillo (copyrighted © December 2012, all rights reserved); reproduced here with photographer's permission

- Page 55: *Llandanwg Beach* (Wales, United Kingdom), B&W photograph by William Warby (21 September 2018); reproduced under Creative Commons license, Attribution 2.0 Generic (CC BY 2.0):

  https://creativecommons.org/licenses/by/2.0/legalcode

- Page 63: *Clouds*, cropped version of photograph copyrighted © 2019, all rights reserved, by Ilsy Murillo; image reprinted here from *KYSO Flash* online (Issue 12, Summer 2019) with photographer's permission

List of Poems and Stories in Alpha Order

	Title	Genre	Page
1.	A Cold Autumn	Prose poem	22
2.	A Long Broken Passage	Poem	47
3.	An Offering	Poem	32
4.	Elegy Within Earshot of Howling	Poem	52
5.	Letter to a Distant Friend	Poem	17
6.	Oblivion	Poem	24
7.	Old School	Prose poem	35
8.	Overdue Rant	Poem	25
9.	Probity	Poem	44
10.	Pura Vida: An Alternative Travel Guide	Flash fiction	49
11.	Southern Gothic	Poem	13
12.	Still Life With Cocaine and Spiders *	Poem	28
13.	Synchronized Swimmers	Poem	54
14.	Taste	Flash fiction	29
15.	The Calm	Poem	15
16.	The Cold Space	Poem	34
17.	The Dogs of His Life	Poem	36
18.	The Fibonacci Lawn	Poem	12
19.	The Multitudes	Poem	43
20.	The Painter's Garden	Flash fiction	11
21.	The Perfect Spiral	Poem	41
22.	The Premonition	Poem	37
23.	The Winter Sidewalks of Former Lovers *	Poem	46
24.	Things Have Dropped From Me	Flash fiction	19
25.	This Animal	Prose poem	23
26.	Too Long in the Tropics	Poem	21
27.	Two Brothers	Poem	40
28.	Vivid Dreams Again *	Poem	31
29.	Winter Thoughts	Prose poem	45

indicates previously unpublished works

Synchronized Swimmers | 63

Clouds

About the Editor

Clare MacQueen served as webmaster and copy editor for 18 issues of *Serving House Journal* from its launch online in 2010 to its retirement in 2018. She co-edited *Steve Kowit: This Unspeakably Marvelous Life* (Serving House Books, 2015). She's also co-editor, webmaster, and publisher of *KYSO Flash*, the online literary journal she created in 2014 to celebrate a smorgasbord of short-form writings and visual art. Via KYSO Flash Press, she has designed and produced 18 books, including anthologies and collections for writers and artists whose works have appeared in *KYSO Flash* online. Her own essays, reviews, stories, and poems have have appeared in, among others, *New Flash Fiction Review, Ribbons, Serving House Journal, Skylark,* and in the anthologies *Best New Writing 2007* (Hopewell Publications) and *Winter Tales II: Women on the Art of Aging* (Serving House Books, 2012).

www.kysoflash.com

*an online literary journal &
a micro-press of printed books*

Knock-Your-Socks-Off Art and Literature

KYSO Flash is a trademark registered ® 2014 by Clare MacQueen. The KYSO Flash logo is copyrighted © 2015 by Clare MacQueen and was designed in collaboration with James Fancher. All rights reserved.

www.ingramcontent.com/pod-product-compliance
Lightning Source LLC
Chambersburg PA
CBHW051553010526
44118CB00022B/2696